Draw a line to help the girl find her way to t

Connect the dots 1-10 to complete the picture. Start at the ★. Color the picture.

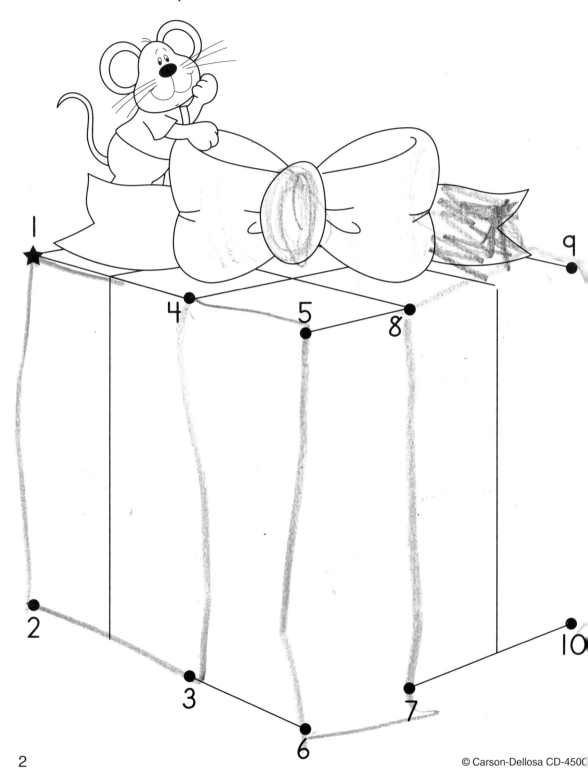

Color by number to see a fun party decoration.

1 = blue   2 = pink

Draw a line from each party hat to the one that matches it.
Color the matching hats the same.

Look at the top picture. Finish the bottom picture so that it looks the same. Color the pictures.

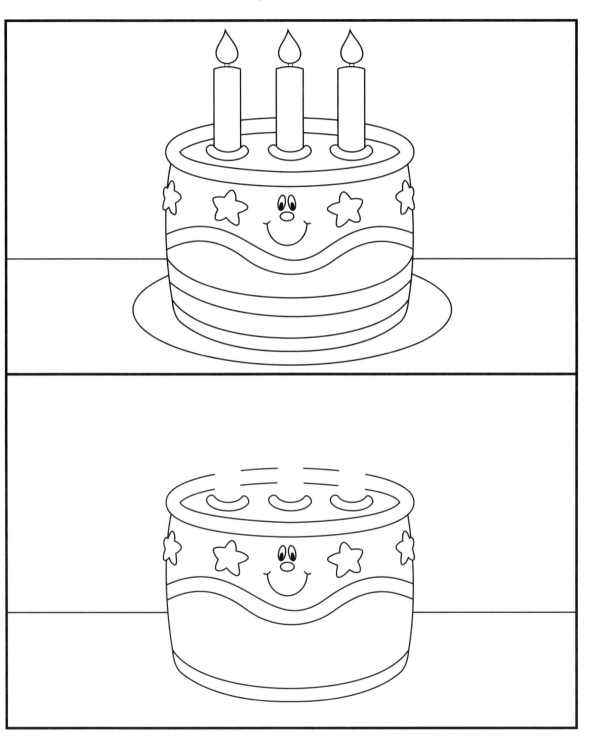

Use the secret code to solve the riddle.

What did the crab's mother make him for his birthday?

$\overline{\triangle}$ $\overline{\bigcirc}\,\overline{\ominus}\,\overline{\triangle}\,\overline{\square}$

$\overline{\bigcirc}\,\overline{\triangle}\,\overline{\heartsuit}\,\overline{\star}$!

Secret Code

$\bigcirc$ = R $\triangle$ = A $\square$ = B

$\heartsuit$ = K $\bigcirc$ = C $\star$ = E

Find and circle the birthday food words from the word list in the puzzle.

g e k p i z z a d y f d
a j h a m b u r g e r s
v o m x g c x c y w m u
p b c e o a u a c n f c
u t h b j e p k s o d a
n x i c e c r e a m r n
h a p u a i w h q p y d
l g s i u y q v l z g y
q i h o t d o g s k n g
a b w r c x s o

Word List

| cake | chips | hot dogs | pizza |
| candy | hamburgers | ice cream | soda |

Find and color these shapes in the picture. Color the picture.

♡ = red   □ = orange   △ = green   ◯ = yellow

Draw a line to match each toy on the left to the package on the right that is the correct shape.

Decorate and color the cake. Remember to add candles!

Find and circle the five children hiding at this surprise party. Color the picture.

Color the picture.

Draw a line to help the boy find the piñata.

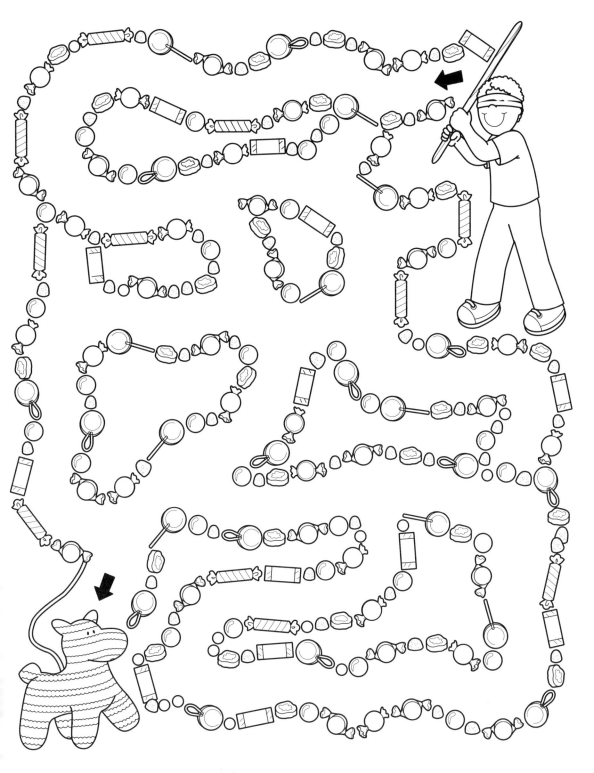

Unscramble the letters to write the name of each birthday item shown.

 a t h   h _ _ _

 f t g i   g _ _ _ _

 n a y c d   c a _ _ _ _

 k a c e   c _ _ _ _

 o c w l n   c _ _ _ w _

14

Connect the dots 1-10 to complete the picture. Start at the ★. Color the picture.

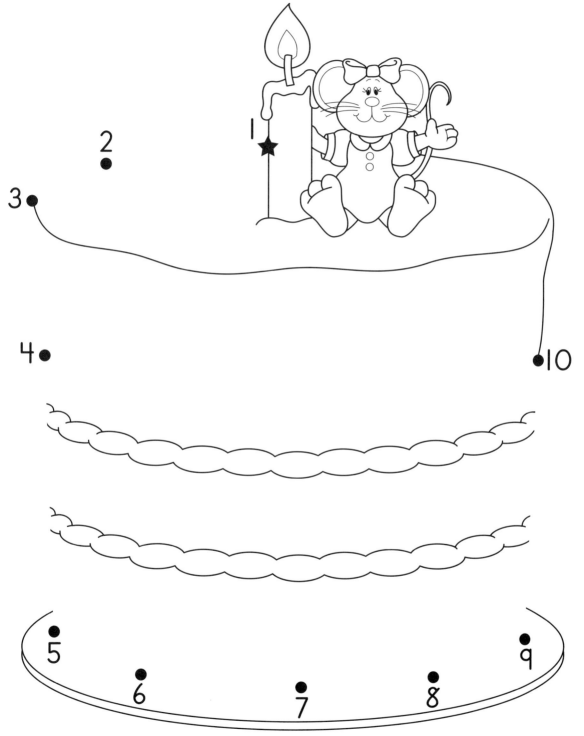

Draw a line from each birthday cake to the one that matches it. Color the matching cakes the same.

Color by number to see a birthday treat.

1 = yellow   2 = green   3 = purple

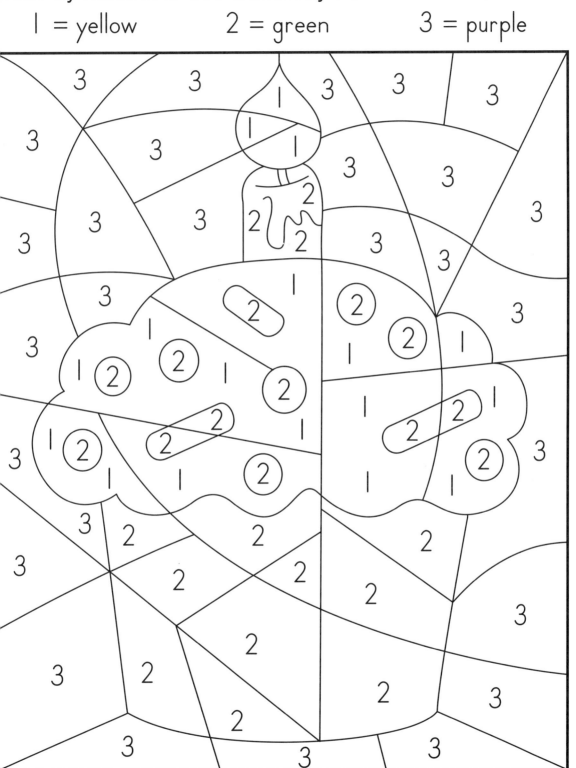

Color the picture.

Use the secret code to solve the riddle.

What is the best thing to put in a birthday cake?

Secret Code

⬭ = R   △ = U   □ = T   ♡ = H

○ = O   ▭ = E   ☆ = Y

© Carson-Dellosa CD-4500

19

Use the words from the word list to solve the crossword puzzle.

Word List

balloons games

candles presents

Across

3. The birthday child gets lots of _____.

4. Colorful _____ are favorite party decorations.

Down

1. Children at birthday parties play fun _____.

2. The birthday child blows out the _____.

Find and circle five . Color the picture.

Find and circle the birthday words from the word list in the puzzle.

```
i  b  f  r  i  e  n  d  s  u
r  v  s  f  j  d  d  a  s  i
d  e  c  o  r  a  t  e  g  k
p  l  f  o  k  c  c  w  t  t
r  s  f  d  m  u  m  u  x  j
e  u  p  a  r  t  y  l  d  h
s  l  e  l  v  p  d  c  e  a
e  r  q  n  u  z  o  a  i  p
n  i  g  d  p  p  n  r  e  p
t  o  b  i  r  t  h  d  a  y
```

Word List

birthday	decorate	friends	party
card	food	happy	present

Color the picture.

Find and circle the two candies that are the same. Color the picture.

Draw a line to find the way through the cake.

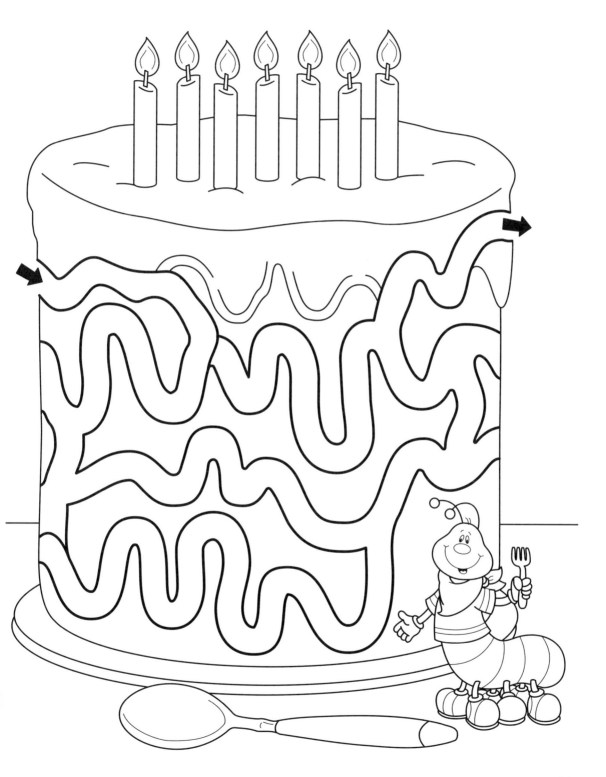

Design and color your own birthday wrapping paper for this present.

26

Unscramble the birthday words. Use the word list if you need help. Then, write the circled letters in order on the lines below to solve the riddle.

1. s i h w ⬭◯ __ __ __

2. s s r u r p i e __ __ __ __ __ ◯ __ __

3. t e s n s r e p __ __ __ __ __ __ ◯ __

4. s h t a ◯ __ __ __

5. l s e c n a d __ ◯ __ __ __ __ __ __

6. r y a t p __ __ __ __ ◯ __

How does every birthday end?

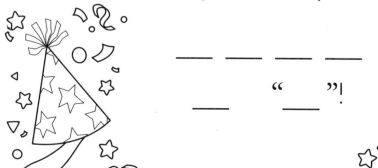

__ __ __ __

" __ __ __ "!

Word List

candles

hats

party

presents

surprise

wish

© Carson-Dellosa CD-4500

27

Look at the top picture. Finish the bottom picture so that it looks the same. Color the pictures.

Connect the dots 1-15 to complete the picture. Start at the ★. Color the picture.

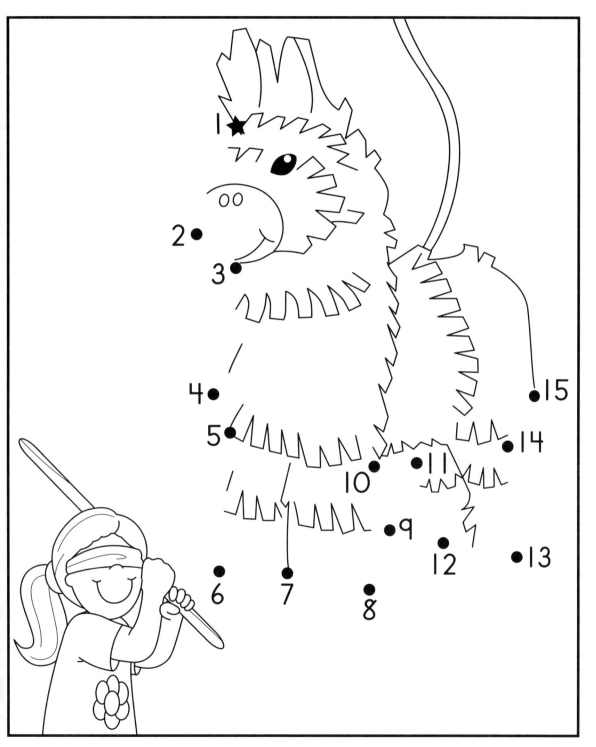

Color by number to see a birthday gift.

1 = blue   2 = brown   3 = pink   4 = green

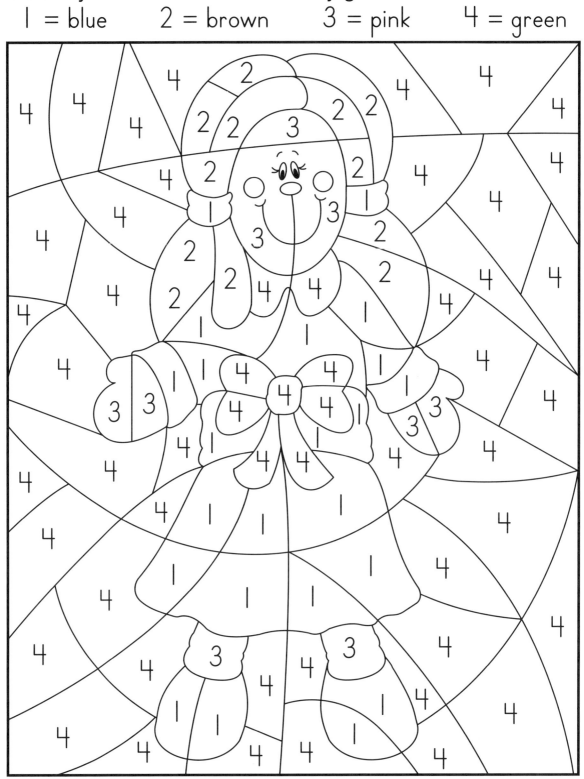

Birthday Puzzles and Games Answer Key

Page 1
The maze should be completed.

Page 2
The picture should be a gift.

Page 3
The picture should be a pink balloon on a blue background.

Page 4

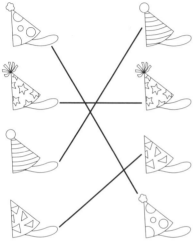

Page 5
The candles, icing, and plate should be drawn.

Page 6   A CRAB CAKE!

Page 7

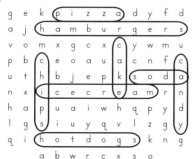

Page 8
The heart balloon should be red, the circle balloons yellow, the square gifts orange, and the triangle hat and box flaps green.

Page 9

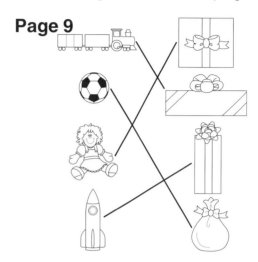

Page 10
Pictures will vary.

Page 11
The children are hidden behind the couch, behind the drapes, under the table, and behind the door.

Page 12
The picture should be colored.

Page 13
The maze should be completed.

Page 14
hat   gift
candy   cake
clown

Page 15
The picture should be a cake.

A

Page 16

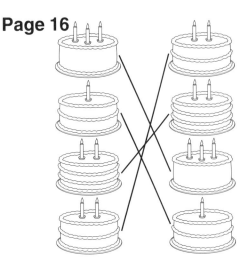

Page 17
The candle, cupcake paper, and sprinkles should be green, the icing and flame yellow, and the background purple.

Page 18
The picture should be colored.

Page 19   YOUR TEETH!

Page 20
Across	Down
3. presents	1. games
4. balloons	2. candles

Page 21
The candles are hidden in the girl's braid, on her skirt, as a donkey tail, as part of the wall design along the baseboard, and at the end of the baseball bat.

Page 22

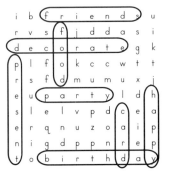

Page 23
The picture should be colored.

Page 24

Page 25
The maze should be completed.

Page 26   Pictures will vary.

Page 27
| 1. wish | 2. surprise | 3. presents |
| 4. hats | 5. candles | 6. party |

WITH A "Y"!

Page 28
The whipped cream, toppings, and sprinkles should be drawn.

Page 29
The picture should be a piñata.

Page 30
The doll's hair should be brown, her face, legs, and hands pink, her shoes and dress blue, her bow, collar and the background green.

Page 31
Across	Down
3. invitations	1. wish
5. hats	2. happy
	4. older

Page 32

Page 33

The stars on the hat, cake and sugar should be red, the rectangles as cabinet doors, butter, and apron pocket orange, the diamonds on the hair bow and cake green, and the ovals on the spoon, cake top, and as eggs yellow.

Page 34   AT THE FLEA MARKET!

Page 35

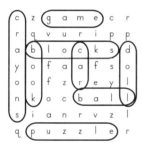

Page 36

The maze should be completed.

Page 37

The clown's nose and cheeks, the flower on the hat, the dots on the bow tie, the elbow patch, and the shirt and cuff buttons should be drawn.

Page 38

The picture should be colored.

Page 39
1. sing   2. balloons   3. cupcakes
4. fun   5. friends   6. ice cream
7. special   8. games

Page 40
The gift should be purple, the ribbon yellow, and the background orange.

Page 41
The picture should be a clown.

Page 42
Across   Down
4. ice cream   1. cake
                          2. wrap
                          3. candy
                          5. card

Page 43
The gifts are hidden on the chimney, the windows, on the door, and on the right side of the roof.

Page 44
The picture should be colored.

Page 45   WITH TOMATO PASTE!

Page 46

Page 47

The maze should be completed.

Page 48

1. hot potato
2. Simon says
3. hokey pokey
4. musical chairs
5. hide and seek

Page 49

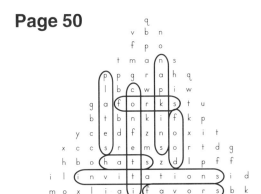

Page 50

Page 51

Across	Down
2. sings	1. clown
5. birthday	3. surprise
	4. party

Page 52

Pictures will vary.

Page 53

The ice cream should be yellow and pink, the cone brown, and the background green.

Page 54

THEY WERE YELLING SURPRISE!
D

Page 55

The ribbons, bows, and strips should be drawn.

Page 56

The picture should be a balloon.

Page 57

1. birthday
2. family
3. happy
4. favor
5. confetti
6. cards
7. older
8. invite
I'M PRESENT

Page 58

The slice of cake is a hat on the girl's head, the baseball is a balloon, the camera is in the tablecloth pattern, the crayon is on one of the boy's pant legs, the ice cream cone is part of a balloon one of the boys is holding, the cupcake is in a glass, the party hat is on the other boy's pant leg, and the peppermint candy is a balloon.

Page 59

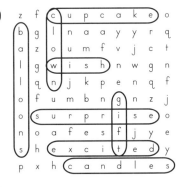

Page 60

Across	Down
2. decorate	1. blow
4. fun	2. dance
	3. age

Use the words from the word list to solve the crossword puzzle.

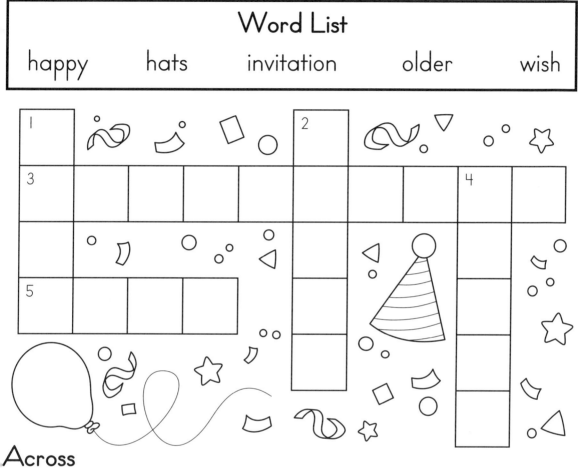

Word List				
happy	hats	invitation	older	wish

Across

3. Send an _____ to ask friends to come to a party.

5. Sometimes people wear birthday party _____.

Down

1. You get to _____ when you blow out the candles.

2. The first word of the birthday song is _____.

4. Each birthday, you get a year _____.

Draw a line to connect each pair of birthday objects that belong together.

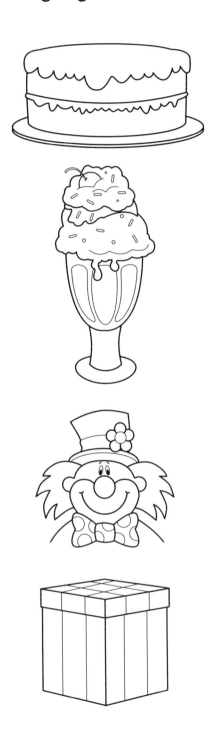

Find and color these shapes in the picture. Color the picture.

☆ = red   ▭ = orange   ◇ = green   ⬭ = yellow

Butter

Star

Sugar

33

Use the secret code to solve the riddle.

Where can you buy a birthday present for your dog?

$\overline{}\ \overline{}\quad\overline{}\ \overline{}\ \overline{}$
2   8   8   1   3

$\overline{}\ \overline{}\ \overline{}\ \overline{}$
6   4   3   2

$\overline{}\ \overline{}\ \overline{}\ \overline{}\ \overline{}\ \overline{}$!
7   2   9   5   3   8

Secret Code

1 = H	2 = A	3 = E	4 = L	5 = K
6 = F	7 = M	8 = T	9 = R	

Find and circle the birthday present words from the word list in the puzzle.

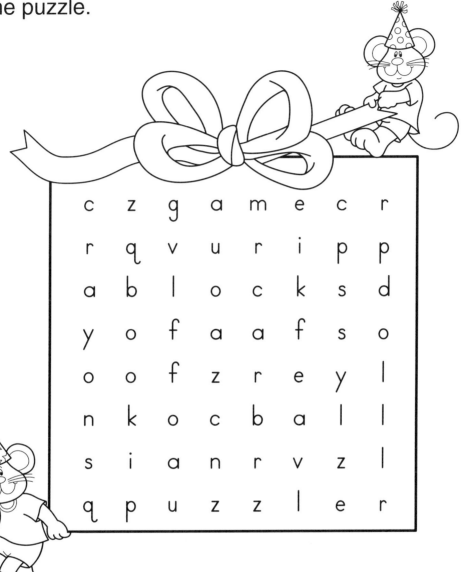

c	z	g	a	m	e	c	r
r	q	v	u	r	i	p	p
a	b	l	o	c	k	s	d
y	o	f	a	a	f	s	o
o	o	f	z	r	e	y	l
n	k	o	c	b	a	l	l
s	i	a	n	r	v	z	l
q	p	u	z	z	l	e	r

Word List

ball	book	crayons	game
blocks	car	doll	puzzle

Draw a line to help the kids find the way to the birthday party.

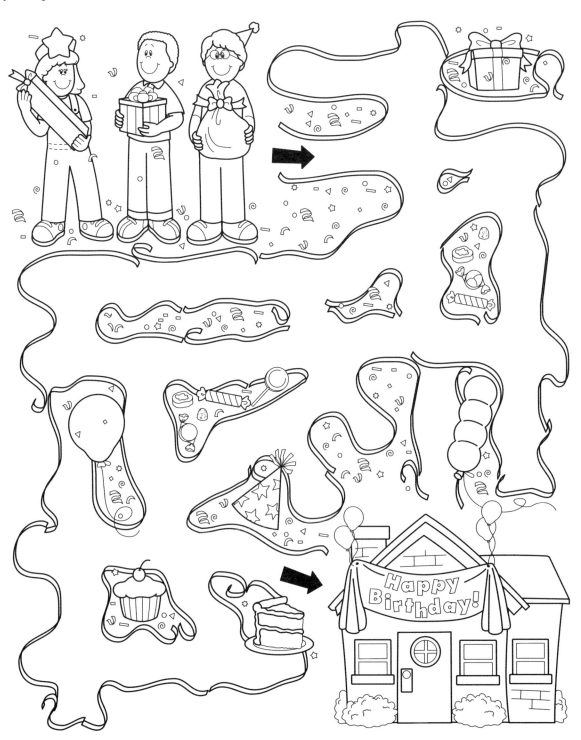

36

Look at the top picture. Finish the bottom picture so that it looks the same. Color the pictures.

Draw a design on the clown's costume. Then, color the picture.

38

Unscramble the birthday words. Use the word list for help.

1. s g i n __ __ __ __

2. s l o a n b l o __ __ __ __ __ __ __ __

3. c k s c u a p e __ __ __ __ __ __ __ __

4. n f u __ __ __

5. d r f e i n s __ __ __ __ __ __ __

6. c e i m r c e a

   __ __ __ __ __ __ __ __

7. i e p s l a c __ __ __ __ __ __ __

8. s m a g e __ __ __ __ __

Word List			
balloons	friends	games	sing
cupcakes	fun	ice cream	special

Color by number to see a surprise.

1 = orange   2 = purple   3 = yellow

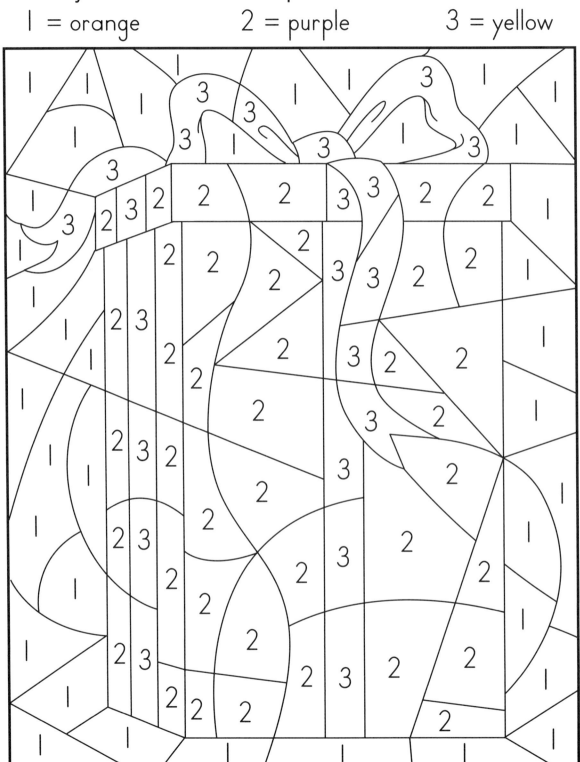

Connect the dots 1-20 to complete the picture. Start at the ★. Color the picture.

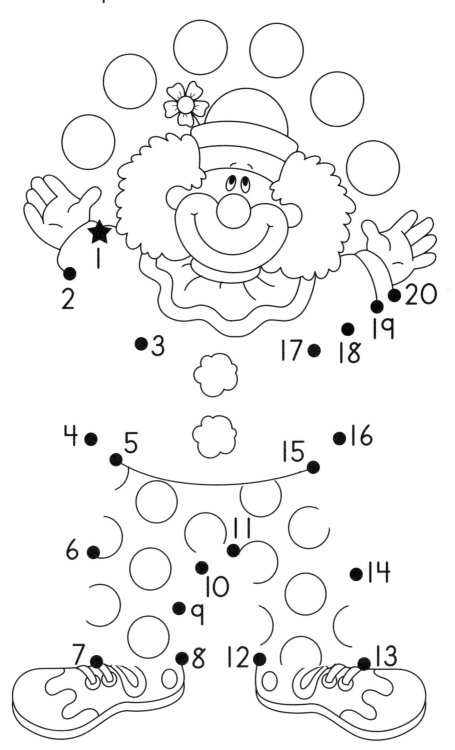

Use the words from the word list to solve the crossword puzzle.

Word List

| cake | candy | card | ice cream | wrap |

Across

4. A cold treat that goes with cake is _____ .

Down

1. You put the candles on the _____ .
2. Before you give someone a present, you _____ it.
3. When you break a piñata, _____ comes out.
5. It is nice to send a birthday _____ to your friend.

Find and circle six . Color the picture.

Color the picture.

Use the secret code to solve the riddle.

How did Katie fix the broken pizza
at her birthday party?

$\overline{}$ $\overline{}$ $\overline{}$ $\overline{}$
 2   10   4   7

$\overline{}$ $\overline{}$ $\overline{}$ $\overline{}$ $\overline{}$ $\overline{}$
 4   9   3   6   4   9

$\overline{}$ $\overline{}$ $\overline{}$ $\overline{}$ $\overline{}$!
 1   6   8   4   5

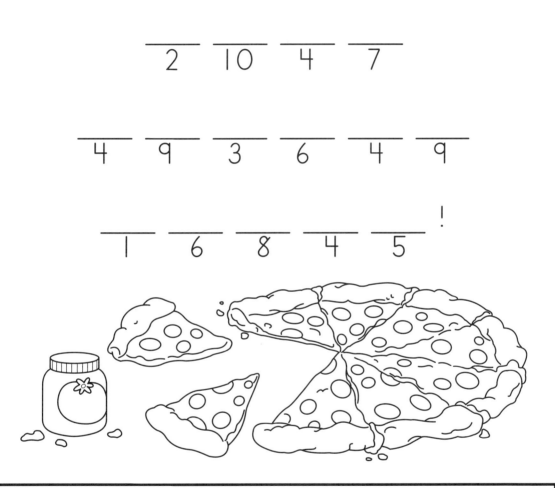

Secret Code

1 = P	2 = W	3 = M	4 = T	5 = E
6 = A	7 = H	8 = S	9 = O	10 = I

Find the two pictures that are the same. Color them the same.

46

Draw a line to find the way through the gift.

Unscramble the birthday games. Use the word list for help.

1. tho opttoa ___ ___ ___

   ___ ___ ___ ___ ___ ___

2. nSmio yssa ___ ___ ___ ___ ___

   ___ ___ ___ ___

3. eokyh opeky ___ ___ ___ ___ ___

   ___ ___ ___ ___ ___

4. iuclmsa rhisca

   ___ ___ ___ ___ ___ ___ ___

   ___ ___ ___ ___ ___ ___

5. deih nda kese ___ ___ ___ ___

   ___ ___ ___ ___ ___ ___ ___

Word List

hokey pokey	hide and seek	musical chairs
	hot potato	Simon says

Find and circle the shadow that matches the mouse.

Find and circle the birthday party words from the word list in the puzzle.

```
              q
        v   b   n
        f   p   o
     t   m   a   n   s
   p   p   g   r   a   h   q
   l   b   c   w   p   i   w
 g   a   f   o   r   k   s   t   u
 b   t   b   n   k   i   f   k   p
 y   c   e   d   f   z   n   o   x   i   t
x  c   c   s   r   e   m   s   o   r   t   d   g
h  b   o   h   a   t   s   z   d   l   p   f   f
i  l   i   n   v   i   t   a   t   i   o   n   s   i   d
m  o   x   l   i   a   i   f   a   v   o   r   s   b   k
```

Word List

confetti	food	hats	napkins
favors	forks	invitations	plates

Use the words from the word list to solve the crossword puzzle.

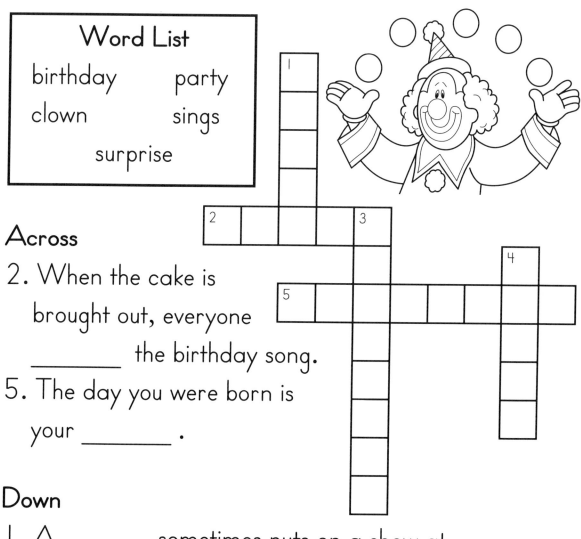

Word List

birthday   party

clown   sings

surprise

Across

2. When the cake is brought out, everyone _____ the birthday song.

5. The day you were born is your _____ .

Down

1. A _____ sometimes puts on a show at birthday parties.

3. A birthday party for someone who doesn't know about it is called a _____ party.

4. When people get together to celebrate a birthday, it's called a _____ .

Draw a picture in the box of a birthday present you would like to get. Color the picture.

Color by number to see a cool treat.

1 = brown   2 = yellow   3 = pink   4 = green

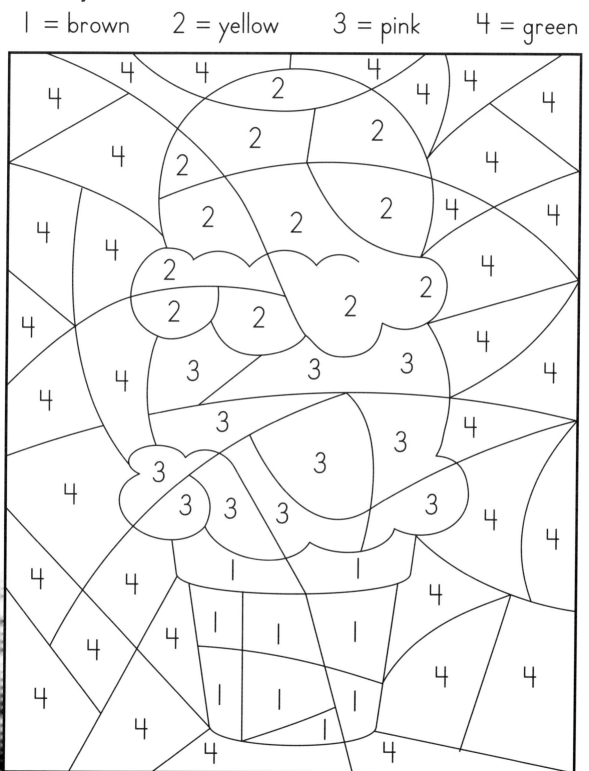

Use the secret code to solve the riddle.

Why did everyone yell at John at his birthday party?

__4__ __7__ __5__ __9__ __2__ __5__ __12__ __5__

__9__ __5__ __11__ __11__ __10__ __3__ __13__

" __8__ __6__ __12__ __1__ __12__ __10__ __8__ __5__ ! "

Secret Code

1 = P	2 = W	3 = N	4 = T	5 = E
6 = U	7 = H	8 = S	9 = Y	10 = I
	11 = L	12 = R	13 = G	

Look at the top picture. Finish the bottom picture so that it looks the same. Color the pictures.

Connect the dots 1-20 to complete the picture. Start at the ★. Color the picture.

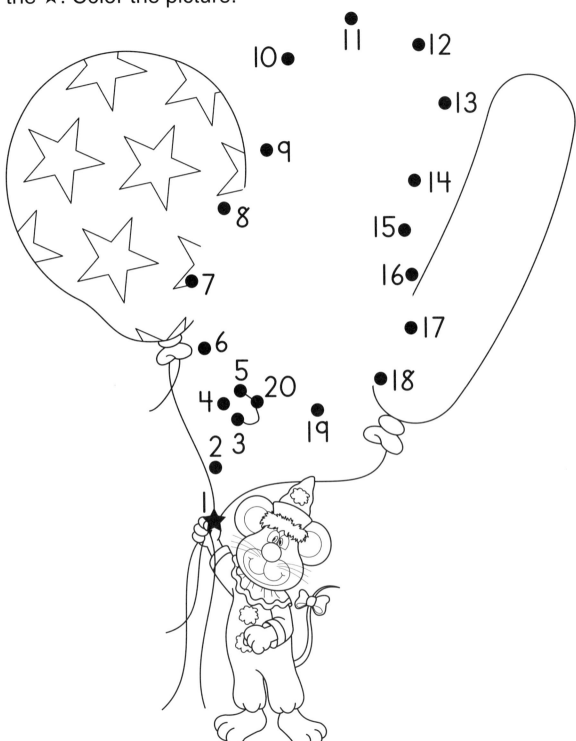

Unscramble the birthday words. Then, write the circled letters in order on the lines below to answer the riddle.

1. d t i b r a h y   b ◯ _ _ _ _ d _ _

2. i a l y f m   f _ ◯ _ l _

3. p y p h a   _ _ _ p ◯ _

4. o a r v f   _ a _ _ ◯

5. t t o n f e c i   c _ _ _ _ ◯ _ _ i

6. d r c a s   _ _ _ _ d ◯

7. l r o d e   o _ _ ◯ r

8. n i t e v i   _ ◯ v _ ◯ _

What did the gift say when it got to the birthday party?

_ _   _   _ _ _ _ _ _ , _ _ _ _ _

Find and circle these items in the picture: slice of cake, baseball, camera, crayon, ice cream cone, cupcake, party hat, peppermint candy. Color the picture.

Find and circle the birthday party words from the word list in the puzzle.

z	f	c	u	p	c	a	k	e	o
b	g	l	n	a	a	y	y	r	q
a	z	o	u	m	f	v	j	c	t
l	g	w	i	s	h	n	w	g	n
l	q	n	j	k	p	e	n	q	f
o	f	u	m	b	n	g	n	z	j
o	s	u	r	p	r	i	s	e	o
n	o	a	f	e	s	f	j	y	e
s	h	e	x	c	i	t	e	d	y
p	x	h	c	a	n	d	l	e	s

Word List

balloons	clown	excited	surprise
candles	cupcake	gift	wish

Use the words from the word list to solve the crossword puzzle.

Word List

age   blow   dance   decorate   fun

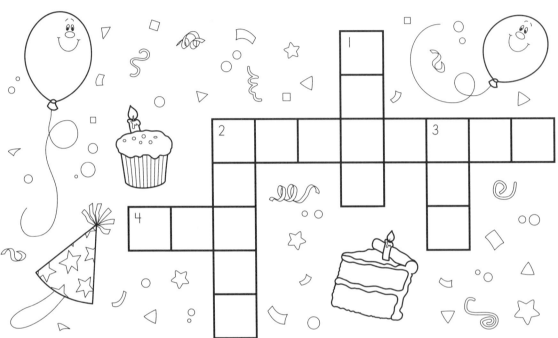

Across

2. It is fun to _____ with streamers for a party.
4. Birthday parties are lots of _____!

Down

1. To make a wish, _____ out the candles!
2. At some parties you play music and _____.
3. On your birthday, people want to know your _____.

60   © Carson-Dellosa CD-4500